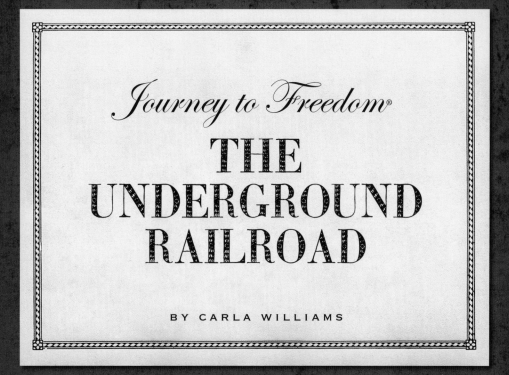

Journey to Freedom®

THE UNDERGROUND RAILROAD

BY CARLA WILLIAMS

"I HAVE HEARD THEIR GROANS AND SIGHS, AND SEEN THEIR TEARS, AND I WOULD GIVE EVERY DROP OF BLOOD IN MY VEINS TO FREE THEM."

~ HARRIET TUBMAN ~

Cover and page 4 caption:
Slaves who worked on
plantations lived together
in cabins.

Content Consultant:
Richard Cooper, Interpretive
Services, Education
Department, National
Underground Railroad
Freedom Center

Published in the United States of America by The Child's World®
1980 Lookout Drive, Mankato, MN 56003-1705
800-599-READ • www.childsworld.com

ACKNOWLEDGEMENTS

The Child's World®: Mary Berendes, Publishing Director

The Design Lab: Kathleen Petelinsek, Design; Gregory Lindholm, Page Production

Red Line Editorial: Amy Van Zee, Editorial Direction

PHOTOS

Cover and page 4: Bettmann/Corbis

Interior: AP Images, 6, 11; Bettmann/Corbis, 14; Charles Webber/AP Images, 9; H. B. Lindsley/
Library of Congress, 12; James E. Taylor/Library of Congress, 25; Joshua Smith/AP Images, 17;
Kean Collection/Getty Images, 23; Library of Congress, 5, 15, 22, 24; Louie Psihoyos/Corbis, 21;
North Wind Picture Archives, 16, 18, 19, 20; Paul Warner/AP Images, 27; Theodore R. Davis/
Library of Congress, 7; William Manning/Corbis, 26

LIBRARY OF CONGRESS CATALOGING-IN-PUBLICATION DATA

Williams, Carla, 1965-

  The Underground Railroad / by Carla Williams.

     p. cm. — (Journey to freedom)

  Includes bibliographical references and index.

  ISBN 978–1–60253–139–0 (library bound : alk. paper)

  1. Underground Railroad—Juvenile literature. 2. Fugitive slaves—United States—History—19th
century—Juvenile literature. I. Title.

  E450.W7 2009

  973.7'115—dc22

                                  2008031946

CONTENTS

Ships arrive bringing captured Africans to Jamestown (modern-day Virginia) in 1619.

Chapter One

SLAVERY AND ABOLITION

There are many stories, myths, and legends about the Underground Railroad. So what exactly was it? The Underground Railroad was a secret system of safe houses used to help **enslaved** blacks reach freedom. Before slavery became illegal in the United States, the Underground Railroad was an important network of people who believed that all humans had the right to be free. They worked to make that idea a reality.

Hundreds of years ago, men and women from different parts of Africa were taken from their homelands. They were captured forcefully and enslaved. Slave traders brought them to North America and to other lands. The first Africans arrived in North America in 1619. Over time, all 13 American colonies legalized slavery.

Captive Africans were brought across the Atlantic Ocean on large ships. They were put in dark, cramped spaces in the bottoms of the ships. These Africans were chained together and forced to lie on wooden planks. They were not allowed to stand up or to move about. Those who became ill were thrown into the ocean to drown. An estimated 1 to 2 million enslaved Africans died during these difficult journeys across the Atlantic.

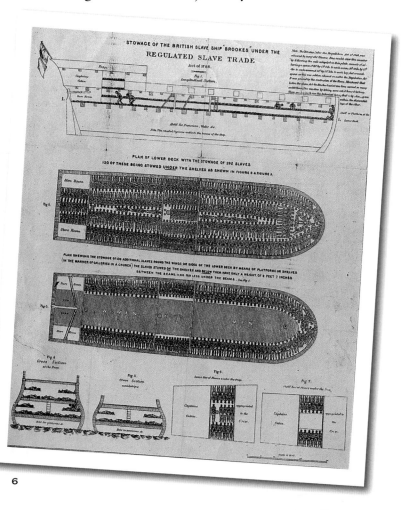

This diagram shows how slaves were "stowed" on ships during the journey across the Atlantic Ocean. This journey was called the Middle Passage.

At slave auctions, captured blacks were sold for the highest bid and usually separated from their families.

When the Africans got off the ships, they were sold at public **auctions** to the highest bidders. They were separated from their families. Most never saw their loved ones again.

By the 1800s, enslaved men, women, and children were often sent to work on plantations in the Southern states. Plantations were large farms owned by white people. The Northern states had fewer farms and many Northern states had fewer slaves.

Slaves were forced to work long hours for no pay. They were bought and sold as needed. They were not considered to be human beings, and they had no rights. Slave masters beat and sometimes killed their slaves. The slave masters were not punished because slaves were considered personal property.

Many slaves tried to escape from their owners. But the slave owners wanted to keep the slaves to work on their plantations and farms. In 1850, a law called the **Fugitive** Slave Act made it illegal for slaves to escape. Under this law, escaped slaves could be captured and returned to their owners. Even if the slaves reached the Northern states, they were not safe. If they were caught and sent back, they were usually punished severely. Despite the dangers, many slaves still tried to escape. They believed it was better to seek freedom and risk being caught than to stay in a life of slavery.

The people who wanted to end slavery were called **abolitionists**. They believed that slavery was wrong and fought to change the laws that allowed it. Some abolitionists helped slaves escape and others sheltered escaped slaves. However, the Fugitive Slave Act also made it a crime for anyone to help slaves escape. If the abolitionists were caught doing this, they could be punished.

Not every black person in the United States was a slave. There were also free black people; most of them lived in the North and the West. Black people could become free in several different ways. Some abolitionists bought slaves just to set them free. Some slave owners freed their own slaves. Other times, free blacks bought freedom for family members who were still enslaved. And some free blacks had never been enslaved. Free blacks carried special papers or passes to prove their freedom.

This illustration by Charles Webber shows abolitionists aiding escaped slaves.

Many free black people were also abolitionists. They wanted to end the suffering of enslaved blacks.

Abolitionists developed a loose system of safe houses, trails, and secret codes for slaves to follow to make their way to freedom. This system became known as the Underground Railroad.

Setting up and maintaining the Underground Railroad was not easy. Communication was difficult. There were no telephones, and slaves were not allowed to learn how to read or write. Some slaves learned in secret, but most could not read even a simple message.

Slaves could not hold meetings. Information about escaping came to them either in secret or in code. Information about the Underground Railroad traveled by word of mouth. The system worked because it was flexible. The Underground Railroad workers were very clever. Sometimes they helped slaves escape by leaving clues out in plain sight. Because the clues were in secret codes, the slave owners could not understand them.

When did people begin using the phrase "Underground Railroad"? One night in 1831, an enslaved man named Tice Davids escaped from Kentucky. To get to the free state of Ohio, he swam across the Ohio River. When he got to the Ohio side, he disappeared. His owner searched for Davids but never saw him again. The owner told his friends that Davids "must have gone off on an underground road." Years later, a reporter said that a captured slave talked

Before slavery was abolished in the United States, more than 100,000 slaves escaped to freedom with help from the Underground Railroad system.

about a "railroad that went underground all the way to Boston." The name Underground Railroad comes from these stories. "Underground" meant that it was secret. "Railroad" meant that it was a way to travel from one point to another. It was a hidden way to escape from slavery to freedom.

A "station" on the Underground Railroad in Wilton, Connecticut

Harriet Tubman was a nurse in the **Union** army.

Chapter Two

AGENTS, STATIONMASTERS, AND CONDUCTORS

Workers on the Underground Railroad were skilled at hiding slaves and transporting them to freedom. Thousands of people aided the Underground Railroad system. Some people gave abolitionist groups money to buy food and clothing for the escaped slaves. Others went to the South to guide the slaves to the North. Some people opened their homes to fugitive slaves. This was very dangerous. If a person was caught hiding slaves, he or she would be punished.

Most of the people who were part of the Underground Railroad were not famous. These people worked hard and were very brave. They gave themselves titles used by workers on real railroads, and each person had a different job to do. Agents helped slaves escape by giving clues, money, or other help. Stationmasters took escaped slaves into their homes (which were called "stations") to hide them. Conductors guided escaped slaves on their journeys.

But some Underground Railroad workers became very well known. Harriet Tubman was born into slavery in Maryland around 1821. She worked as a field hand. When she was a child, her master often beat her. But Harriet was strong. One day, a scuffle broke out when another slave ran off. The **overseer** who watched over the slaves threw a heavy iron object at the runaway slave—but it hit Harriet in the head instead. For the rest of her life, Harriet had a deep scar on her forehead and often had painful headaches.

In 1849, Tubman found out that she and her brothers were going to be sold to another owner. She decided to escape. Her brothers and her husband, John, were afraid to try to escape, but Tubman was not. At age 28, she walked alone from Maryland to Pennsylvania. Even though she was free, Tubman was not happy. She missed her family. Tubman decided that they should all be free with her. So she worked in the North and saved her pay. Then she used the money to go back and get her family. First, Tubman freed her sister and her sister's children. Then she went back and helped one brother and two other men escape.

Harriet Tubman's injury also caused her to faint without notice.

Harriet Tubman helped many members of her family escape to freedom. But when she went back for her husband, he was afraid to come. She left him behind.

Harriet Tubman (left) with slaves whom she helped escape

Harriet Tubman went back to the South more than ten times. She helped most of her family to freedom, including her aged parents, her brothers and sisters, and their families. Like many escaped slaves, Tubman's family went to Canada. Because of the Fugitive Slave Act, the Northern states were not completely safe. But the U.S. laws did not apply to Canada. Enslaved men, women, and children also fled to Mexico and the Caribbean.

Tubman was tough. She would not let anyone slow her down. In fact, she carried a gun—not to protect herself, but to force the fugitives to keep moving forward. If the slaves she was helping tried to turn back, she threatened to shoot them. She knew that anyone who turned back could tell **bounty hunters** where to find her and the other fugitives. They might even reveal secrets about the Underground Railroad. Despite her threats, Tubman never had to shoot anyone. And no one she helped ever went back to slavery.

Tubman became one of the Underground Railroad's most famous conductors. Slave owners offered large rewards for her capture. Even with the big scar on her forehead, Tubman was never recognized.

Frederick Douglass was born into slavery in Maryland around 1817. His owner allowed him to work for other people and to keep part of his pay. Douglass did not spend his hard-earned money.

Harriet Tubman saved so many people from slavery and led them to freedom that she was called the "Moses of Her People."

A portrait of abolitionist Frederick Douglass

Abolitionist Levi Coffin
opened his home to
help escaped slaves.

Instead, he saved every penny so that one day he could escape. In 1838, Douglass escaped to Massachusetts. There he met and worked with abolitionists.

Douglass had a deep, beautiful voice. He became a famous speaker. He even traveled to England to speak against slavery. He published the story of his life so that people would know about the terrible treatment of slaves.

Douglass settled in Rochester, New York. He published a newspaper about the abolitionist movement called the *North Star*.

He reached many people through his speeches and writing. Rochester is very close to the Canadian border. Douglass became an Underground Railroad stationmaster, which meant his home was a stop for escaped slaves on their way to freedom. Frederick and his wife, Anna Murray Douglass, helped dozens of escaped slaves reach Canada.

Some of the people who helped the Underground Railroad system had never been enslaved. Levi Coffin was a white man born in the Southern state of North Carolina. From a young age, he believed that slavery was wrong.

When Levi was a boy, he and his father saw a group of slaves chained together. Levi's father asked the slaves why they were chained. They said it was so they could not return to their families. Another day, Levi's father spoke with a slave. The slave was beaten just for talking to him. Levi never forgot these things.

Later in life, Levi and his wife, Catharine, moved to Newport, Indiana, and became abolitionists. Their house was known as the "Grand Central Station" of the Underground Railroad. The Coffins later moved to Cincinnati, Ohio, but they continued to help escaped slaves. No slave who stayed with the Coffins was ever captured or returned to slavery. Because of this, Levi Coffin was called the "President" of the Underground Railroad.

It is believed that Levi Coffin helped more than 3,000 slaves escape to freedom in Indiana and Ohio.

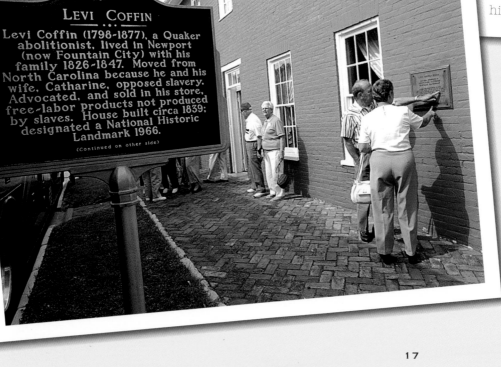

LEVI COFFIN

Levi Coffin (1798–1877), a Quaker abolitionist, lived in Newport (now Fountain City) with his family 1826–1847. Moved from North Carolina because he and his wife, Catharine, opposed slavery. Advocated, and sold in his store, free-labor products not produced by slaves. House built circa 1839; designated a National Historic Landmark 1966.

(Continued on other side)

Levi Coffin's home in Fountain City, Indiana, is now a historical site.

Most slaves escaped on foot, sometimes through swamps.

Chapter Three

CREATIVE ESCAPES

ost slaves had only one way to escape—by walking. They traveled through the woods at night so they would not be seen. To reach freedom, many slaves had to walk hundreds of miles. Sometimes their shoes wore out, forcing them to walk barefoot the rest of the way. Sometimes they had to cross deep rivers and streams. Escaping slaves were cold, hungry, and tired. Their feet ached. Even so, they kept going. They knew that freedom lay ahead.

Some workers for the Underground Railroad found creative ways to help slaves escape. Many of these stories are known today because of William Still. He was a black man who had been born free in Philadelphia, Pennsylvania. He worked for the Underground Railroad. Mr. Still could read and write. He kept daily records of Underground Railroad activity and wrote down the stories of the men and women who escaped through Philadelphia. He later published these stories.

Some slaves figured out their own ways to escape, but they still made use of the Underground Railroad. William and Ellen Craft were married slaves in Georgia. William was a cabinetmaker and a hotel waiter. Ellen was a seamstress. Ellen was a very light-skinned slave. In fact, she was sometimes mistaken for a white woman.

Ellen came up with a plan. Near the end of 1848, she had William buy her a men's suit. Ellen would pretend to be a white man. She wore high-heeled boots and a high hat to look taller. She wrapped her head in a handkerchief and claimed to have a toothache. The handkerchief kept people from seeing her face too closely and noticing that she did not have any whiskers.

William pretended to be Ellen's servant. Black servants often traveled with their white masters, so no one thought it was strange. They were able to stay in nice hotels because the owners thought Ellen was white. Ellen could not read or write, so she wrapped her hand in a sling and pretended it was hurt. That way, she did

Much of what is known about the Underground Railroad comes from the writings of William Still.

Ellen Craft was careful not to speak when she escaped with her husband. Her voice would have revealed that she was in disguise.

THE

UNDERGROUND RAIL ROAD.

A RECORD

OF

FACTS, AUTHENTIC NARRATIVES, LETTERS, &c.,

Narrating the Hardships Hair-breadth Escapes and Death Struggles

OF THE

Slaves in their efforts for Freedom,

AS RELATED

BY THEMSELVES AND OTHERS, OR WITNESSED BY THE AUTHOR;

TOGETHER WITH

SKETCHES OF SOME OF THE LARGEST STOCKHOLDERS, AND

MOST LIBERAL AIDERS AND ADVISERS,

OF THE ROAD.

BY

WILLIAM STILL,

For many years connected with the Anti-Slavery Office in Philadelphia, and Chairman
of the Acting Vigilant Committee of the Philadelphia Branch of
the Underground Rail Road.

Illustrated with 70 fine Engravings by Bensell, Schell and others, and
Portraits from Photographs from Life.

Thou shalt not deliver unto his master the servant that has escaped from his master unto thee.—*Deut.* xxiii. 15.

SOLD ONLY BY SUBSCRIPTION.

PHILADELPHIA:

PORTER & COATES,

822, CHESTNUT STREET.

1872.

The title page from Still's record of the Underground Railroad, published in 1872 not have to sign her name at the hotels. The Crafts went to Boston, but soon their old master found them. He sent bounty hunters to bring them back. But the Crafts refused to go back to slavery. Abolitionists helped them get out of town, and they settled in England, where slavery was illegal. Once slavery was outlawed in the United States, William and Ellen Craft returned.

Dressing as a boy brought another young woman to freedom. Anna Maria Weems was just 15 years old when she escaped from slavery in Washington DC. Anna knew that a girl traveling alone would attract attention. She also knew that if she ran away, her owners would report the escape of a young girl. So Anna dressed as a boy. No one noticed her, and she escaped to Philadelphia. Her owner offered a $500 reward for her capture, but she was not caught. From Philadelphia, Anna made her way to New York. She later went to Canada, where she was able to go to school.

Several slaves were actually mailed to freedom in boxes. Henry Brown was a slave in Virginia who wanted to be free.

A poster offering a reward for a runaway slave

$200 Reward.

Ranaway from the subscriber, last night, a mulatto man named FRANK MULLEN, about twenty-one years old, five feet ten or eleven inches high. He wears his hair long at the sides and top, close behind, and keeps it nicely combed; rather thick lips, mild countenance, polite when spoken to, and very genteel in his person. His clothing consists of a variety of summer and winter articles, among which are a blue cloth coat and blue casinet coatee, white pantaloons, blue cloth do., and a pair of new ribbed casinet do., a blue Boston wrapper, with velvet collar, several black hats, boots, shoes, &c. As he has absconded without any provocation, it is presumed he will make for Pennsylvania or New-York. I will give one hundred dollars if taken in the State of Maryland, or the above reward if taken any where east of that State, and secured so that I get him again, and all reasonable expenses paid if brought home to the subscriber, living in the city of Washington.

October 21, 1835.   **THOS. C. SCOTT.**

Lear Green was a young woman who also mailed herself to freedom. She was packed into a sailor's chest and ended up at the home of Underground Railroad worker William Still.

In 1849, he planned a way to be mailed to Philadelphia. His friend Samuel Smith was a white carpenter. Henry ordered a box from Smith. The box was big enough for Henry to fit inside. Henry climbed into the box, bringing a little water and a few biscuits with him for the journey. Smith addressed the box to abolitionist headquarters in Philadelphia. He marked it, "This Side Up With Care." But not every postal worker set the box upright, and Henry spent much of the trip on his head. The box was sometimes handled roughly. After 26 hours in the box, Henry arrived safely in Philadelphia. He earned the nickname "Box" because of his clever escape. Henry "Box" Brown went to work for the Underground Railroad in Boston. Samuel Smith was later sent to prison for building crates for two other slaves.

A drawing portraying Henry "Box" Brown and his clever escape

MEN OF COLOR
To Arms! To Arms!
NOW OR NEVER
THREE YEARS' SERVICE!
AND JOIN IN FORMING THE
BATTLES OF LIBERTY AND THE UNION
FAIL NOW, & OUR RACE IS DOOMED

Posters like this one recruited black men to the Union army.

Chapter Four

AND FREEDOM FOR ALL

In 1861, the Southern states fired on Fort Sumter, a federal fort in South Carolina. This act marked the beginning of the **U.S. Civil War**. The Union army fought for the Northern states, and the **Confederate** army fought for the Southern states. One reason for the war was that no one could agree on the issue of slavery. While the United States was still expanding as a country, many Northerners did not want to extend slavery to these new regions. Southerners, however, wanted to make slavery legal in the new parts of the nation.

Harriet Tubman and Frederick Douglass worked for the Union army. Tubman was a nurse and a spy. Douglass encouraged black men to join

More than 200,000 black men fought in the Civil War. Most of them had been formerly enslaved.

the Union army. Douglass was also a friend of President Abraham Lincoln. He often talked to President Lincoln about **emancipation**.

Lincoln declared the Confederacy's slaves free on January 1, 1863, when he signed the Emancipation Proclamation. But this law did not truly free the slaves because the Confederate states no longer considered themselves part of the United States. They refused to accept such a demand from the U.S. president. For two more years, war and slavery continued. Many cities in the North and South were destroyed as battles tore through the country. Finally, in 1865, Confederate General Robert E. Lee **surrendered**, and the war soon ended. Later that year, slavery was made illegal by the Thirteenth **Amendment** to the U.S. **Constitution**. There was no longer a need for the Underground Railroad.

It has been well over a century since slavery was abolished in the United States, but people still remember and honor the Underground Railroad. It is an important part of U.S. history. Family stories are handed

A sketch of a school set up to educate freed slaves after the Civil War

24

The National Underground Railroad Freedom Center in Cincinnati, Ohio

down from generation to generation. Perhaps one of your ancestors worked on the Underground Railroad. Perhaps the system helped one of your ancestors escape to freedom.

In 1990, the U.S. Congress asked the National Park Service to study the history of the Underground Railroad. In 2000, President Bill Clinton signed the National Underground Railroad Freedom Center Act. This act set aside $16 million to restore important historical sites and develop educational programs to teach people about this turning point in U.S. history. Today, many of the Underground Railroad sites are museums.

People can still follow some of the routes and visit homes that were part of the Underground Railroad. Historian Anthony Cohen decided to trace the route that some slaves took to freedom. In 1996, he started out in Maryland and walked 800 miles (1287 km) to Canada. On some days, he walked as many as 37 miles (60 km). He walked through the states of Maryland, Pennsylvania, and New York. It took him six weeks.

In 1998, Cohen walked from Alabama to Canada, tracing another route of the "freedom train."

It took most escaped slaves much longer than that to reach freedom. Unlike Cohen, they could not walk in the daylight. They did not always have food, shelter, or warm clothing as he did. But they did not give up. Cohen walked in their footsteps and honored the amazing strength and courage of the ordinary people who did extraordinary things to help one another be free.

Many supporters walked along with Anthony Cohen for portions of his journey.

TIME LINE

| 1600 | 1700 | 1800 | 1820 | 1830 |

1619
Dutch slave traders land in Virginia and bring the first Africans to the American colonies.

1775
The first abolitionist group in the United States is founded in Philadelphia.

1798
Abolitionist Levi Coffin is born in North Carolina. As a child, he sees injustice against black people that encourages him to fight slavery.

1808
The slave trade is abolished.

1826
Levi and Catharine Coffin move to Newport, Indiana, where they live for more than 20 years. Their house becomes a station for the Underground Railroad.

1838
Frederick Douglass escapes from slavery.

1840 | **1850** | **1860** | **1900** | **2000**

1847
Douglass publishes the first issue of the *North Star* newspaper, which provides information about the abolitionist movement.

1848
Ellen and William Craft escape to freedom and arrive in Pennsylvania on Christmas Day.

1849
Harriet Tubman escapes to freedom. Henry "Box" Brown is mailed to freedom in a wooden box.

1850
The Fugitive Slave Act passes and provides for the return of runaway slaves to their owners. Anyone who helps slaves escape can be punished.

1850
Harriet Tubman makes her first trip back to the South. Aided by the Underground Railroad, she helps slaves escape to freedom.

1861
The U.S. Civil War begins.

1863
On January 1, President Abraham Lincoln signs the Emancipation Proclamation, which declares all slaves in the Confederate states to be free. The Southern states reject it.

1865
The Civil War ends. Slavery is abolished in the United States by the Thirteenth Amendment to the U.S. Constitution.

1868
Ellen and William Craft return to the United States.

1990
The U.S. Congress asks the National Park Service to study the history of the Underground Railroad so that monuments can be identified and preserved.

1996
Historian Anthony Cohen traces an Underground Railroad route. He walks 800 miles (1287 km) from Maryland to Canada.

1998
Anthony Cohen traces an Underground Railroad route from Alabama to Canada.

2000
President Bill Clinton signs the National Underground Railroad Freedom Center Act. This sets aside $16 million to restore historic sites on the routes and create educational programs.

GLOSSARY

abolitionists
*(ab-uh-**lish**-uh-nists)*
Abolitionists were people who worked to abolish slavery before the Civil War. Abolitionists believed that slavery was wrong and fought to change the laws that allowed it.

amendment
*(uh-**mend**-munt)*
An amendment is a change that is made to a law or legal document. The Thirteenth Amendment to the Constitution ended slavery in the United States.

auctions
*(**awk**-shunz)*
Auctions are sales in which items are sold to people who offer the most money. Slaves were sold at auctions.

bounty hunters
*(**bown**-tee **hunt**-urz)*
Bounty hunters are people who are rewarded for catching fugitives. Bounty hunters tracked and captured escaped slaves.

Confederate
*(kun-**fed**-ur-uht)*
The Confederate states were the Southern states that left the Union in 1860 and 1861. The Confederate states wanted to maintain the practice of slavery.

Constitution
*(kon-stuh-**too**-shun)*
The Constitution is the written document containing principles by which the United States is governed. Slavery was outlawed by an amendment to the U.S. Constitution.

emancipation
*(ih-man-sih-**pay**-shun)*
Emancipation is the act of freeing a person or group from slavery or control. The Emancipation Proclamation in 1863 declared all slaves in the Confederate states to be free.

enslaved
*(en-**slayvd**)*
When people are enslaved, they are forced to be slaves or are owned by other people. People who are enslaved lose their freedom.

fugitive
*(**fyoo**-juh-tiv)*
A fugitive is a person who is running away from something, especially the law. The Fugitive Slave Act of 1850 made it illegal to help slaves escape to freedom.

overseer
*(**oh**-vur-see-er)*
An overseer is a person who supervises others as they work. As a young girl, Harriet Tubman was hit in the head with a heavy object thrown by an angry overseer.

surrendered
*(suh-**ren**-durd)*
If an army surrendered, it gave up to its enemy. Confederate General Robert E. Lee surrendered to the Union army in 1865.

Union
*(**yoon**-yun)*
The Union is another way of referring to the United States. During the Civil War, Union referred to the Northern states.

U.S. Civil War
*(u s **siv**-il **wor**)*
The U.S. Civil War was fought between the North and the South from 1861 to 1865. One result of the Civil War was the abolition of slavery in the United States.

FURTHER INFORMATION

Books

Ashby, Ruth. *Underground Railroad*. Mankato, MN: Black Rabbit Books, 2003.

Hansen, Joyce, and Gary McGowan. *Freedom Roads: Searching for the Underground Railroad*. Chicago: Cricket Books, 2003.

Hossell, Karen Price. *The Emancipation Proclamation*. Chicago: Heinemann Library, 2005.

Weatherford, Carole Boston. *Moses: When Harriet Tubman Led Her People to Freedom*. New York: Hyperion Books, 2006.

Welch, Catherine A. *Frederick Douglass*. New York: Barnes & Noble, 2002.

Videos

Underground Railroad. Host Alfre Woodard. Triage, Inc., 1999.

A Woman Called Moses. Dir. Paul Wendkos. Perf. Cicely Tyson, Orson Welles. 1978. Xenon, 2001.

Web Sites

Visit our Web page for links about the Underground Railroad:

http://www.childsworld.com/links

NOTE TO PARENTS, TEACHERS, AND LIBRARIANS: We routinely verify our Web links to make sure they are safe, active sites—so encourage your readers to check them out!

Index